THE EPIGRAMS OF
RALPH WALDO EMERSON

INTRODUCTION AND
EDITED BY ERIC BRITON

Fredonia Books
Amsterdam, The Netherlands

The Epigrams of Ralph Waldo Emerson

by
Ralph Waldo Emerson

Introduction and edited by Eric Briton

ISBN: 1-58963-915-4

Fredonia Books
Amsterdam, The Netherlands
http://www.fredoniabooks.com

CONTENTS

> *Work of his hand*
> *He nor commends nor grieves :*
> *Pleads for itself the fact ;*
> *As unrepenting Nature leaves*
> *Her every act.*

> *If we meet no gods, it is because we harbour*
> *none.*

INTRODUCTION

THE epigram, a monumental inscription, as the ancient Greeks understood and conceived it, became associated at a later period in Western Europe with the abusive and satirical writings of the wits and savants, and was employed as a vehicle of invective against persons or parties. It is no small tribute to the genius of more recent literary effort that it has restored epigram to higher and nobler uses.

In the earlier writings of Emerson the virility of his mind is evidenced by the incisive and arrestive quality of his style. It is cryptic, enigmatic, and forceful, and compels the reader to think over and weigh his words with care. The subject upon which he wrote had been exhaustively studied and pondered over, until he was enabled to illuminate it with the clear white light of a warm-blooded and affectionate genius. "There was a man behind the book," to use his own words in writing on Goethe.

The essays of Emerson are punctuated and made still more precious by the happy use of pure epigram in a style peculiarly his own. There is a recurring fondness for apposition of terms, as seen in "Hitch your wagon to a star" and "The Eden of God is bare and grand." The essays (in prose) are often set forth with a wealth of poetic diction and allusion; whilst the poems are conceived chiefly in the rugged form and vigour of the old Norse saga, and are to be valued as the lapidary values uncut gems, not for their form, but for their intrinsic worth. At the same time one of the finest examples of pure epigram is found among the poems in the following lines from "Woodnotes":

> Thou canst not wave thy staff in air,
> Or dip thy paddle in the lake,
> But it carves the bow of beauty there,
> And the ripples in rhymes the oar forsake.

Emerson has sometimes been called a "Transcendentalist," this title being intended to convey a somewhat vague idea of the foolish vapouring of an unpractical and tremulous mind: a kind of literary and philosophic epileptic with whose strange aberrations we ought to show a sympathetic patience.

A closer study of the writings of Emerson soon dispels this strange fallacy, and reveals the crystal purity and purpose of this living stream of the Divine source of all things. We feel the surprised delight of the woman at the well on a memorable occasion, and are impelled to seek out and ask our friends to come and see the man who has written all that ever we thought or tried to think about and were unable to utter.

After tasting these samples of the living water the reader may be induced to imbibe deeper draughts from this refreshing stream of high thoughts and exalted aims.

In placing these extracts under classified heads the terms of the various headlines have been construed in their widest sense. No item is placed under more than one head, although it might with propriety have been included under another, or under two or three other different groups.

To those who lack the leisure and opportunity to engage in a more detailed study of the voluminous writings of the great philosopher it is hoped this collection of his literary gems may prove of interest and value.

ERIC BRITON

LIFE AND MORALS

LIFE'S LESSONS, AIMS, AND OBJECTS
LIFE MAGICAL, MUSICAL
A FACT AND A FANTASY
LIFE A LYRIC, AN EPIC, A POEM OR ROMANCE
MORALITY AND CONSISTENCY
CHEERFULNESS AND A HEALTHY MIND
SELF-TRUST AND SELF-HELP
JUSTICE AND DEBT : VIRTUE AND GENIUS
FATALISM AND HEROISM
VALUE OF MONEY. POWER. HEALTH. AND WEALTH

LIFE AND MORALS

PLATO is philosophy, and philosophy Plato.

Involuntarily we always read as superior beings.

The world exists for the education of each man.

Every reform was once a private opinion.

∽

We cannot strongly state one fact without seeming to belie some other.

Life is a succession of lessons which must be lived to be understood.

Life only is good when it is magical and musical.

I do not wish to expiate, but to live.

∽

My life is for itself and not for a spectacle.

Life itself is a bubble and a scepticism, and a sleep within a sleep.

Life is a series of surprises, and would not be worth taking or keeping if it were not.

Life is not worth the living to do tricks in.

Nothing great was ever achieved without enthusiasm.

❦

The best of life is conversation, or perfect understanding between sincere people.

Life may be a lyric or an epic, as well as a poem or a romance.

❦

We acquire the strength we have overcome.

There is no moral deformity but is a good passion out of place.

Life is a boundless privilege.

Life is not so short but there is always time enough for courtesy.

To fill the hour, that is happiness.

❦

Let us be poised and wise and our own to-day!

Never was a sincere word utterly lost.

If you would not be known to do anything, never do it!

The lesson conveyed is Be, not Seem.

Blame is safer than praise.

Drudgery, calamity, exasperation, want, are
instructors in eloquence and wisdom.

Self-trust is the first secret of success.

⤚

Why should you keep your head over your
shoulder? Suppose you should con-
tradict yourself,—what then?

A foolish consistency is the hobgoblin of
little minds, adored by little statesmen,
philosophers, and divines.

⤚

Always scorn appearances and you always
may.

Justice is not postponed.   A perfect equity
adjusts its balance in all parts of life.

Life is a scale of degrees.

The borrower runs in his own debt.

⤚

First or last you must pay your entire debt.

For every benefit you receive a tax is levied.

A little integrity is better than any career.

We have a great deal more kindness than
is ever spoken.

B

My prudence consists in avoidance and
    going without.

Prudence is the virtue of the senses. It is
    content to seek health of body and
    mind.

           *

When you have chosen your part abide by it.

We are wiser than we know.

What a little of all we know is said!

Can anything be so elegant as to have few
    wants and to serve them one's self?

           *

The times are the masquerade of the
    eternities.

To-day is a king in disguise.

The making a fact the subject of thought
    raises it.

           *

Society is a masked ball, where every one
    hides his real character, and reveals
    it by hiding.

Society will pardon much to genius and
    special gifts.

Wit makes its own welcome and levels all
    distinctions.

We must learn by laughter as well as by tears and terrors.

The highest heaven of wisdom is alike near from every point.

⌒

Wonderful intricacy in the web, wonderful constancy in the design, this vagabond life admits.

Our thinking is a pious deception. We have little control over our thoughts. We are the prisoners of ideas.

What is the hardest task in the world? To think!

⌒

Each mind has its own method.

Entire self-reliance belongs to the intellect.

Thought makes everything fit for use.

Everything must be taken genially, and we must be at the top of our condition to understand anything rightly.

⌒

Genius and virtue, like diamonds, are best plain set.

Adaptiveness is the peculiarity of human nature.

The only sin we can never forgive each other is difference of opinion.

Health is the condition of wisdom, and the sign is cheerfulness.

For performance of great mark, it needs extraordinary health.

∽

The healthy state of mind is the love of life.

Repose and cheerfulness are the badge of the gentleman.

A cheerful, intelligent face is the end of culture.

∽

The joy of the spirit indicates its strength.

All healthy things are sweet-tempered.

What is useful will last, what is hurtful will sink.

The best things are of secular growth.

∽

Nothing is more simple than greatness; indeed, to be simple is to be great.

Moral qualities rule the world.

One may be too punctual and too precise.

Real service will not lose its nobleness.

Let us be generous of our dignity, as of our money.

☙

Only that good profits which serves all men.

If solitude is proud, so is society vulgar.

Society and solitude are deceptive names.

Let us not be the victims of words.

☙

The punishment which the wise suffer, who refuse to take part in the government, is to live under the government of worse men.

They are not kings who sit on thrones, but they who know how to govern.

☙

They should own who can administer; not they who hoard and conceal.

Money often costs too much, and power and pleasure are not cheap.

Life is a search after power; no honest seeking goes unrewarded.

Power is the first good.

Health is the first muse.

All high beauty has a moral element in it.

We live by our imaginations, by our admirations, by our sentiments.

As is the receiver so is the gift.

Unconscious creatures do the whole will of wisdom.

Truth is the property of no individual, but is the treasure of all men.

The foundation of culture, as of character, is at last the moral sentiment.

No institution is better than the instituter.

Cities give not the human senses room enough.

If the king is in the palace nobody looks at the walls.

The law is only a memorandum.

Keep the town for occasions, but the habits should be formed to retirement.

Wealth begins in a tight roof that keeps the rain and wind out.

Commerce is a game of skill which every man cannot play; which few men can play well.

Wealth is mental; wealth is moral.

❧

There is no chance in results. The first wealth is health.

A great soul will be strong to live, as well as strong to think.

Give me insight into *to-day*, and you may have the antique and future worlds.

❧

A scholar is the favourite of Heaven and earth, the excellency of his country, the happiest of men.

Every age, like every human body, has its own distemper.

❧

We may be partial, but Fate is not.

It will never make any difference to a hero what the laws are.

The hero is he who is immovably centred.

Every hero becomes a bore at last.

Of all wit's uses, the main one
Is to live well with who has none.

✍

For he that feeds men serveth few;
He serves all who dares be true.

✍

Seeing only what is fair,
Sipping only what is sweet,
Leave the chaff and take the wheat.

✍

Nor kind nor coinage buys
Aught above its rate :
Fear, Craft, and Avarice
Cannot rear a State.

✍

He spoke, and words more soft than
    rain
Brought the Age of Gold again.

✍

The aroma of my life is gone,
Like the flower with which it came.

CHARACTER AND ACTION

CHARACTER AND ACTION

THE force of character is cumulative.

Character is higher than intellect.

Thinking is the function. Living is the functionary.

❧

Do what you know, and perception is converted into character.

That which we are we shall teach not voluntarily, but involuntarily.

Character teaches over our head.

Commanding worth and personal power must sit crowned in all companies.

❧

To be great is to be misunderstood.

We pass for what we are. Character teaches above our wills.

Your genuine act will explain itself. Your conformity explains nothing.

The restraining grace of common sense is the mark of all the valid minds.

27

It is not talent, but sensibility, which is best.

Feel yourself, and be not daunted by things.

Congratulate yourself if you have done something strange and extravagant.

❧

Nothing is beneath you if it is in the direction of your life.

The virtues are economists, but some of the vices are also.

Every advantage has its tax. I learn to be content.

❧

Character and wit have their own magnetism.

The compensations of calamity are made apparent to the understanding after long intervals of time.

What we do *not* call education is more precious than that which we call so.

❧

Nothing seems so easy as to speak and to be understood.

A public oration is an escapade, an apology, not a speech, not a man.

Nothing is at last sacred but the integrity of your own mind.

Expect me not to shew cause why I seek or why I exclude company.

The use of history is to give value to the present hour and its duty.

⌒

Good nature is stronger than tomahawks.

Serving others is serving us.

Activity is contagious.

We are all wise in capacity, though so few in energy.

⌒

What is rich? Are you rich enough to help anybody?

Without the rich heart wealth is an ugly beggar.

Every one must seek to secure his independence, but he need not be rich.

⌒

To be rich is to have a ticket of admission to the masterworks and chief men of each race.

Spend after your genius, and by system.

The true thrift is always to spend on the higher plane.

Be rich to great purposes, poor only for selfish ones.

He only is rich who owns the day.

∽

It is long ere we discover how rich we are.

He is great who confers the most benefits.

To think is to act.   Let me heed my duties.

Day and night, house and garden, a few books, a few actions, serve us as well as would all trades and all spectacles.

∽

Everything good is on the highway.

We thrive by our casualties.

Courage is nothing else than knowledge.

Never mind the ridicule, never mind the defeat ;—up again, old heart.

∽

No change of circumstances can repair a defect of character.

Character is centrality.   A man should give us a sense of mass.

Grandeur of character works in the dark, and succours them who never saw it.

Self-respect is the early form in which greatness appears.

❧

Self-respect is our practical perception of the Deity in man.

Accept that work for which you were inwardly formed.

Let your feet run, but your mind need not.

❧

Our spontaneous action is always the best.

We do not want actions, but men.

A strenuous soul hates cheap successes.

It is enough if you work in the right direction.

❧

The time is never lost that is devoted to work.

Do your work, respecting the excellence of the work, and not its acceptableness.

Intellectual tasting of life will not supersede muscular activity.

Do not craze yourself with thinking, but go about your business anywhere.

Work is victory. Wherever work is done, victory is obtained.

～

Do your work and I shall know you.
Do your work and you shall re-enforce yourself.

Whenever you are sincerely pleased, you are nourished.

～

Be lord of a day through wisdom and justice, and you can put up your history books.

Our words and actions to be fair must be timely.

There is no calamity which right words will not begin to redress.

～

If you would lift me, you must be on higher ground.

If you would liberate me, you must be free.

We know better than we do.

Success treads on every right step.

Heroism feels and never reasons, and therefore is always right.

Hospitality must be for service and not for show.

Sport is the bloom and glow of perfect health.

⌀

If I cannot work, at least I need not lie. Cannot we screw our courage to patience and truth?

You cannot do wrong without suffering wrong.

⌀

There are days which are the carnival of the year.

Every day is the best day in the year.

Every day is Doomsday.

Do not refuse the employment which the hour brings you.

⌀

What I do is all that concerns me, not what people think.

Beware of too much good staying in your hand. Pay it away quickly in some sort.

Commit a crime and the earth is made of glass.

C

For the angel Hope aye makes
Him an angel whom she leads.

His tongue was framed to music,
And his hand was armed with skill,
His face was the mould of beauty,
And his heart the throne of will.

On bravely through the sunshine or the
    showers,
Time has his work to do, and we have ours.

FRIENDSHIP AND LOVE

FRIENDSHIP AND LOVE

THERE are two elements that go to the composition of friendship: one is truth, and the other is tenderness.

Better be a nettle in the side of your friend than his echo.

∾

There must be very two before there can be very one.

We must be our own before we can be another's.

Wait and thy heart shall speak.

A man's friends are his magnetisms.

∾

The things that are really for thee gravitate to thee.

The only reward of virtue is virtue; the only way to have a friend is to be one.

Friends such as we desire are dreams and fables.

With friends, as with books, I would have them where I can find them, but seldom use them.

37

The essence of friendship is total magnanimity and trust.

Happy is the house that shelters a friend.

～

The ornaments of a house are the friends who frequent it.

We must know our friends under ugly masks. The calamities are our friends.

Between simple and noble persons there is always a quick intelligence.

～

As we are, so we associate.

Our intellectual and active powers increase with our affection.

We over-estimate the conscience of our friend.

Almost all people descend to meet. All association must be a compromise.

～

When there is sympathy, there needs but one wise man in a company, and all are wise.

Our chief want in life is somebody who shall make us do what we can.

Make yourselves necessary to somebody.

We say things we never thought to have said.

A word warm from the heart enriches me.

❧

If we are related we shall meet.

A friend is the hope of the heart.

The goods which belong to you gravitate to you.

Whilst we converse with what is above us, we do not grow old but grow young.

❧

We know each other very well. We are all discerners of spirits.

Love, and you shall be loved.

Everything is superficial and perishes but love and truth only.

❧

He who is in love is wise, and is becoming wiser.

The sharpest-sighted hunter in the universe is Love.

The affections are the wings by which the intellect launches on the void, and is borne across it.

We must be lovers, and at once the impossible becomes possible.

The sweets of life are not shown except to sympathy and likeness.

The law of love and justice alone can effect a clean revolution.

∽

He forms his friendship with the flowers
Whose habits or whose hue may please him
    best.

∽

A day for toil, an hour for sport,
But for a friend is life too short.

∽

Askest "How long thou shalt stay?"
Devastator of the day!

∽

Give all to love. Obey thy heart. Nothing
    refuse.
Heartily know,—when half-gods go, the gods
    arrive.

∽

I saw bright eyes, fair forms, complexions
    fine,
But not a single soul that spoke to mine.

Cupid goes behind all law,
And Right unto himself does draw,
Unheeded Danger near him strides,
Love laughs, and on a lion rides.

Lover of all things alive,
Wonderer at all he meets,
Wonderer chiefly at himself,
Who can tell him what he is?

MAN

MAN'S PLACE IN NATURE
PHYSICAL AND MENTAL POWERS AND ATTRIBUTES
WEAKNESS AND STRENGTH
DEBTS, DUTIES, AND OBLIGATIONS
AFFECTIONS AND AVERSIONS
INFLUENCE AND EXAMPLE
GIFTS AND ACCOMPLISHMENTS
VICES AND VIRTUES

MAN

ACCEPT the place the Divine Providence has found for you.

Tantalus is but a name for you and me.

Whoso would be a man must be a nonconformist.

❧

A boy is in the parlour what the pit is in the playhouse: he gives an independent, genuine verdict.

No man had ever a defect that was not somewhere made useful to him.

Every man in his lifetime needs to thank his faults.

❧

By self-help man, like the wounded oyster, mends his shell with pearl.

Our strength grows out of our weakness.

A great man is always willing to be little.

The mob is man voluntarily descending to the nature of the beast.

Man's life is a progress, not a station.

45

Each man has his own vocation.   The talent is the call.

The man may teach by *doing*, and not otherwise.

❧

A man passes for that he is worth.

A true man is the centre of things.   Where he is, there is Nature.

Every true man is a cause, a country, and an age.

❧

An institution is the lengthened shadow of one man.

Let a man know his worth, and keep things under his feet.

Welcome evermore to gods and man is the self-helping man.

❧

Insist on yourself, never imitate.

Every great man is a unique.

Men are wiser than they know.

A man cannot speak but he judges himself.

The great man makes the great thing.

MAN

Sensible men are very rare.

Man is a stream whose source is hidden.

Man is the façade of a temple wherein all
wisdom and all good abide.

∽

The soul when it breathes through his
intellect it is genius, through his will
it is virtue, through his affection it is
love.

The key to every man is his thought.

Every man supposes himself not to be fully
understood.

∽

Men cease to interest us when we find
their limitations.

The man is only half himself; the other half
is his expression.

When virtue is in presence, all subordinate
powers sleep.

∽

We need change of objects. Dedication to
one thought is quickly odious.

A man will not be observed in doing that
which he can do best.

We believe in ourselves as we do not believe
in others.

Eloquence shows the power and possibility of man.

The orator is the physician.

The right eloquence needs no bell to call the people together, and no constable to keep them.

❧

The truly eloquent man is a sane man with power to communicate his sanity.

The eloquent man is he who is no beautiful speaker, but who is inwardly drunk with a certain belief.

❧

The highest platform of eloquence is the moral sentiment.

Eloquence is the best speech of the best soul.

Personal force never goes out of fashion.

A gentleman never dodges; his eyes look straightforward.

❧

No house is good for anything without a master.

The first point to courtesy must always be truth.

Every chair should be a throne and hold
  a king.

A gentleman makes no noise, a lady is
  serene.

∽

The flower of courtesy does not bide
  handling.

A man is a golden impossibility.   The line
  he must walk on is a hairsbreadth.

The wise through excess of wisdom is made
  a fool.

∽

The only gift is a portion of thyself.

He is a good man who can receive a gift
  well.

He who knows the most is the rich and
  royal man.

∽

We do not eat for the good of living, but
  because the meat is savoury and the
  appetite is keen.

No man is quite sane,—each has a vein of
  folly in his composition.

Every man of truth, like Plato and Paul,
  does for ever.

D

The education of the general mind never stops.

The highest end of government is the culture of men.

Wild liberty develops iron conscience.

❧

A mob cannot be a permanency.

As long as any man-exists there is some need of him, let him fight for his own.

Every man is wanted, and no man is wanted much.

❧

Every man is a channel through which heaven floweth.

We are as ungrateful as children.

Each man converts some raw material in Nature to human use.

❧

A man is a centre for Nature.

On and for ever onward !

The cheapness of man is every day's tragedy.

Great men exist that there may be greater men.

Man is such as his affection and thought are.

Every man makes his own house and state.

Human strength is not in extremes, but in avoiding extremes.

These strings wound up too high will snap.

⌖

What we have, let it be solid and seasonable and our own.

Man helps himself by larger generalizations.

Great men are distinguished by range and extent.

No great men are original.

⌖

The man co-operates, he loves to communicate.

How can he protect a woman who cannot protect himself?

A sufficient measure of civilization is the influence of good women.

⌖

From time to time in history men are born a whole age too soon.

Eloquence a hundred times has turned the scale of war and peace at will.

Wit has a great charter.

'Tis the measure of a man,—his apprehension of a day.

To answer a question so as to admit of no reply is the test of a man.

⌒

What can you do with an eloquent man?

You may condemn his book, but can you fight against his thought?

There are men who are great only to one or two companions.

⌒

Every man brings into society some particular thought and local culture.

Each man has an aptitude born with him to do easily some feat impossible to any other.   Do your work!

The world is nothing, the man is all.

⌒

The man who renounces himself, comes to himself.

A man in pursuit of greatness feels no little wants.

The chief difference between man and man is a difference of impressionability.

MAN

Every man has a history worth knowing, if he could tell it.

A man is a man only as he makes life and nature happier to us.

❧

Wherever there is power there is age.

Don't be deceived by dimples and curls,—
I tell you that babe is a thousand years old!

No great man ever had a great son.

❧

How shall a man escape from his ancestors?

Men are what their mothers made them.

When each comes forth from his mother's womb, the gate of gifts closes behind him.

We hear eagerly every thought and word quoted from an intellectual man.

❧

A personal influence towers up in memory only worthy.

Man moves in all modes, and stands on tiptoe threatening to hunt the eagle in his own element.

A man must thank his defects, and stand in some terror of his talents.

In youth we clothe ourselves with rainbows, and go as brave as the zodiac.

A man's fortunes are the fruit of his character.

A man must ride alternately on the horses of his private and his public nature.

A good intention clothes itself with sudden power.

A man who knows men, can talk well on politics, trade, law, war, religion.

There is always room for a man of force, and he makes room for many.

Every man is a consumer, and ought to be a producer.

He is the rich man who can avail himself of all men's faculties.

The manly part is to do with might and main what you can do.

A man is the prisoner of his power.

A complete man should need no auxiliaries to his personal presence.

A man already strong is listened to, and everything he says is applauded.

◇

Self-reliance is the basis of behaviour.

The man that stands by himself, the universe stands by him also.

Man is made equal to every event.

Every man's task is his life-preserver.

◇

Nothing is impossible to the man who can will.

The bodies of intemperate men are the tombs of immortal minds.

There is no man who is not indebted to his foibles.

◇

All great men come out of the middle classes.

Men achieve a certain greatness unawares, when working to another aim.

The crowning fortune of a man, is to be born with a bias to some pursuit, which finds him in employment and happiness.

Every man is entitled to be valued by his best moment.

Man is physically as well as metaphysically a thing of shreds and patches.

Nothing so marks a man as imaginative expressions.

Every highly organized person knows the value of social barriers.

The hunger for company is keen, but it must be discriminating and must be economized.

Men are made up of potences. We are magnets in an iron globe.

The perception of the comic is a tie of sympathy with other men, a pledge of sanity.

Our high respect for a well-read man is praise enough of literature.

Each man is a hero and an oracle to somebody.

Every individual man has a new bias which he must obey.

Men are ennobled by morals and by intellect.

If a man would be alone let him look at the stars.

The sensual man conforms thoughts to things; the poet conforms things to his thoughts.

Man is explicable by nothing less than all his history.

All literature writes the character of the wise man.

The difference between men is in their principle of association.

A man is a god in ruins.

I believe man has been wronged; he has wronged himself.

He who does a good deed is instantly ennobled.

So much benevolence as a man hath, so much life hath he.

All men in the abstract are just and good.

All men are poets at heart.

An individual man is a fruit which it cost all the foregoing ages to form and ripen.

A man, a personal ascendancy, is the only great phenomenon.

A man should know himself for a necessary actor.

What is strong but goodness, and what is energetic but the presence of a brave man?

A man was not born for prosperity, but to suffer for the benefit of others.

What is a man born for but to be a reformer, a re-maker of what man has made?

So many promising youths, and never a finished man.

A subtle chain of countless rings
The next unto the farthest brings,
And, striving to be man, the worm
Mounts through all the spires of form.

MAN

Clouded and shrouded, there doth sit
The Infinite embosomed in a man.

＞

A ruddy drop of manly blood
The surging sea outweighs.

＞

This vault which glows immense with light
Is the inn where he lodges for a night.

＞

The richest of all lords is Use,
And ruddy health the loftiest Muse.
Live in the sunshine, swim the sea,
Drink the wild air's salubrity.

＞

Graceful women, chosen men,
Dazzle every mortal.

＞

Oh, what are heroes, prophets, men,—but
   pipes
Through which the breath of Pan doth
   blow
A momentary music.

＞

What is the State ? The hero is the State.
One sage outweighs all China and Japan.

NATURE

A MIRACLE AND A REVELATION
THE RELATION OF NATURE TO MAN
NATURE A VISION OF THE DEITY
INFLUENCE ON MAN'S PHYSICAL AND SPIRITUAL
GROWTH
NATURE'S MAGNIFICENCE AND MINUTENESS
INFLUENCE AND DISCIPLINE
LESSONS AND EXAMPLES
THE UNIVERSAL PRESERVATIVE AND CURATIVE
POWER AND ESSENCE

NATURE

WHO loves Nature? Who does not?

Let us draw a lesson from Nature, which always works by short ways.

Power is in Nature the essential measure of right.

❧

The path of science and of letters is not the way into Nature.

Nature is a mutable cloud which is always and never the same. She hums the well-known air through innumerable variations.

❧

The rich mind lies in the sun and sleeps and is Nature.

In Nature, all is useful all is beautiful.

Nature represents the best meaning of the wisest man.

Nature and books belong to the eyes that see them.

The mid-world is best. Nature as we know her is no saint.

In Nature there are no false valuations.

Character is Nature in the highest form.

❦

Nature does not cocker us ; we are children, not pets.

Nature cannot be surprised in undress.

Nature is loved by what is best in us.

Space exists to divide creatures.

❦

We are encamped in Nature, not domesticated.

Nature is good, but intellect is better.

Nature the dear, best-known face startles us at every turn.

❦

We pity those who can forego the magnificence of Nature for candle-light and cards.

Our life is March weather, savage and serene in one hour.

All things are engaged in writing their history.

In Nature this self-registration is incessant, and the narrative is the print of the seal.

Few substances are found pure in Nature.

Nature protects her own work.

Nature never hurries; atom by atom, little by little, she achieves her work.

On Nature's wheels there is no rust.

Every chance is timed, as if Nature who made the lock knew where to find the key.

The blue sky is a covering for a market, and for the cherubim and seraphim.

An everlasting *Now* reigns in Nature.

Nature is always equal to herself.

Nature is always very much in earnest; her great gifts have something serious and stern.

Nature knows how to convert evil to good.

In Nature all is large, massive repose.

The book of Nature is the book of Fate.

E

The one serious and formidable thing in Nature is a will.

Nature is intricate, overlapped, interweaved and endless.

Nature magically suits the man to his fortunes, by making these the fruit of his character.

A cultivated man, wise to know and bold to perform, is the end to which Nature works.

All power is of one kind, a sharing of the nature of the world.

Power educates the potentate.

Nature requires that each man should feed himself.

For performance Nature has no mercy, and sacrifices the performer to get it done.

Nature is reckless of the individual.   When she has points to carry she carries them.

Life expresses.   Nature tells every secret once.

Nature for ever puts a premium on reality.

Nature has self-poise in all her works.

Nature makes fifty poor melons for one that is good.

Wealth is in application of mind to Nature.

Nature works very hard, and only hits the white once in a million throws.

Nature turns all malfeasance to good.

Nature provides for real needs.

Nature is a rag-merchant, who works up every shred and ort and end into new creations.

Nature wishes that woman should attract man.

Nature on new instruments hums her old tunes.

Nature is the true idealist. She serves us best when, on rare days, she speaks to the imagination.

Nature is the best posture-master.

Nature is a fable whose moral blazes through it.

As language is in the alphabet, so is entire Nature in one atom.

Nature is sanative, refining, elevating.

The solitude of Nature is not so essential as solitude of habit.

∽

Nature, when she adds difficulty, adds brain.

Nature never wears a mean appearance.

Nature never became a toy to a wise spirit.

Nature is a setting that fits equally well a comic or a mourning piece.

∽

Nature stretcheth out her arms to embrace man, only let his thoughts be of equal greatness.

Nature is a discipline of the understanding in intellectual truths.

∽

Nothing in Nature is exhausted in its first use.

The moral influence of Nature upon every individual is that amount of truth which it illustrates to him.

He is great who is what he is from Nature.

Nature is made to conspire with spirit to emancipate us.

Whilst we wait in this Olympus of gods, we think of Nature as an appendix to the soul.

❧

The devotee flouts Nature. I have no hostility to Nature, but a child's love to it. I do not wish to fling stones at my beautiful mother, nor soil my gentle nest.

The aspect of Nature is devout. Like the figure of Jesus, she stands with bended head, and hands folded upon the breast.

❧

The noblest ministry of Nature is to stand as the apparition of God.

We are as much strangers in Nature, as we are aliens from God.

Every day the Sun; and after Sunset, Night and her stars.

❧

In the divine order intellect is primary, Nature secondary.

We can never surprise Nature in a corner.

Nature is unbroken obedience.

We can point nowhere to anything final;
but tendency appears on all hands.

Man must be on his guard against this cup
of enchantments, and must look at
Nature with a super-natural eye.

❧

I draw from Nature the lesson of an intimate
divinity.

The only way into Nature is to enact our
best insight.

Nature will never speak to a dandy.

❧

Dearest Nature strong and kind
Whispered,—"Darling, never mind!"

❧

Spring still makes spring in the mind,
When sixty years are told.

❧

The old wine darkling in the cask
Feels the bloom on the living vine,
And bursts the hoops at hint of Spring.

❧

Spring masks her treasury of heat
Under east-winds crossed with sleet.

NATURE

Four daughters make the family of Time,
But rosy Summer is the darling child.

℃

When Nature falters, fain would zeal
Grasp the felloes of her wheel.

℃

By houses lies a fresher green,
On men and maids a ruddier mien,
As if Time brought a new relay
Of shining virgins every May.

℃

Hast thou named all the birds without a
    gun?
Loved the wood-rose, and left it on its stalk?
O, be my friend and teach me to be thine!

℃

Nature centres into balls,
And her proud ephemerals,
Fast to surface and outside,
Scan the profile of the sphere.

℃

Throb thine with Nature's throbbing breast,
And all is clear from East to West.

℃

He had so sped his wise affairs
That he caught Nature in his snares.

RELIGION

ATTRIBUTES OF THE DEITY, THE HOLY AND
DIVINE
ANCIENT SCRIPTURES AND MYTHOLOGIES
LIVES AND EXAMPLES OF DIVINELY INSPIRED MEN
THE SOUL AND THE DIVINE SPIRIT
INSPIRATION AND CONVENTION
UNITY OF DESIGN AND INFINITY OF FORM
TEMPLES AND CHURCHES
WORSHIP, CREEDS, AND DEEDS
SPIRITUAL RELATION OF MAN AND UNIVERSE
THE VISIBLE AND THE INVISIBLE

RELIGION

ESSENCE or God is not a relation or a part, but the whole.

Prayer is the soliloquy of a beholding and jubilant soul.

To the poet, philosopher, and saint all things are holy, all men divine.

～

Jesus astonishes and overpowers sensual people.

Prometheus is the Jesus of the old mythology.

When gods come amongst men they are not known.

Jesus was not. Socrates and Shakespeare were not.

～

A believing love will relieve us of a vast load of care. Oh my brothers, God exists.

What your heart thinks great, is great. The soul's emphasis is always right.

If I know your sect I anticipate your argument.

75

For non-conformity the world whips you
with its displeasure; therefore a man
must know how to estimate a sour face.

We live in the lap of immense intelligence.

The relations of the soul to the divine spirit
are so pure, that it is profane to seek
to interpose helps.

〜

If we live truly we shall see truly.

Life only avails, not the having lived.

I like the silent church before the service
begins better than any preaching. But
the isolation must not be mechanical,
but spiritual; that is, it must be ele-
vation.

〜

We are afraid of truth, afraid of fortune,
afraid of death, and afraid of each
other.

Every Stoic was a Stoic, but in Christendom,
where is the Christian?

〜

Deal with cause and effect, the chancellors
of God.

Nothing can bring you peace but yourself.

Nothing can bring you peace but the triumph of principles.

By virtue of the Deity thought renews itself inexhaustibly every day.

∽

That soul which within us is a sentiment, outside of us is a law.

There is a crack in everything God has made.

Proverbs are the sanctuary of the intuitions.

Abide in the simple and noble regions of thy life, obey thy heart.

∽

Genius is always ascetic, and piety and love.

How much of human life is lost in waiting ! To-morrow will be like to-day. Life wastes itself while we are preparing to live.

∽

Life is a festival only to the wise.

Never strike sail to a fear. Come into port greatly or sail with God the seas.

Human virtue demands her champions and martyrs.

Our faith comes in moments, our vice is habitual.

The soul that ascends to worship the great God is plain and true.

❧

Beware when the great God lets loose a thinker on this planet. Then all things are at risk.

No facts are to me sacred; none are profane.

❧

God enters by a private door into every individual.

The sublime vision comes to the pure and simple soul in a clean and chaste body.

Divinity is behind our failures, and follies also.

❧

All writing comes by the grace of God,— and all doing and having.

The years teach much which the days never know.

The universe is the bride of the soul.

All private sympathy is partial.

I am very content with knowing,—if only I could know.

Divine persons are character born.

◌

Nature. Here is a sanctity which shames our religions.

Life must be lived on a higher plane.

The soul lets no man go without some visitations and holy days of a diviner presence.

◌

The highest compliment man ever receives from Heaven, is the sending to him its disguised and discredited angels.

There is a power over and behind us, and we are the channels of its communications.

◌

A good soul can by its virtue render the body the best possible.

We are adapted to infinity.

The Eden of God is bare and grand.

God is the bride or bridegroom of the soul.

A world in the hand is worth two in the bush.

We are persuaded that a thread runs through all things.

～

Great believers are always reckoned infidels, impracticable, fantastic, atheistic, and really men of no account.

The world is saturated with deity and with law.

～

Let a man learn to look for the permanent in the mutable and fleeting.

Love is compatible with universal wisdom.

We pray to be conventional, but the wary Heaven takes care that you shall not be, if there is anything good in you.

～

Everything good in man leans on what is higher.

Does the consecration of Sunday confess the desecration of the entire week?

It takes millenniums to make a Bible.

Truth and goodness subsist for evermore.

Don't be a cynic and disconsolate preacher.

Chant the beauty of the good.

The affirmative of affirmatives is love !

Good churches are not built by bad men.

The religion of England is part of good breeding.

❧

The English Church is the church of the gentry. The gospel it teaches is, " By taste ye are saved."

The Church at this moment is much to be pitied. She has nothing left but possession.

❧

Politeness is the ritual of society, as prayers are of the church.

The way of Providence is a little rude.

Every spirit makes its house; but afterwards the house confines the spirit.

❧

If you believe in Fate to your harm, believe it at least for your good.

The revelation of Thought takes man out of servitude into freedom.

F

A breath of will blows eternally through the universe of souls in the direction of the Right and Necessary.

If thought makes free, so does the moral sentiment.

∽

Let us build altars to the Blessed Unity which holds nature and souls in perfect solution.

Let us build altars to the Beautiful Necessity.

∽

Why should we fear to be crushed by savage elements, we who are made up of the same elements?

We may well give scepticism as much line as we can.

∽

We are born loyal.   We are born believing.

God builds his temple in the heart on the ruins of churches and religions.

Heaven always bears some proportion to earth.

The fatal trait is the divorce between religion and morality.

The multitude of the sick shall not make us deny the existence of health.

Forget your books and traditions, and obey your moral perceptions at this hour.

&

There is an intimate interdependence of intellect and morals.

Religion or worship is the attitude of those who see that the nature of things works for truth and right for ever.

&

As we are, so we do. As we do, so it is done to us.

The police and sincerity of the Universe are secured by God's delegating his divinity to every particle.

God has delegated himself to a million deputies.

&

The way to mend the bad world is to create the right world.

To make our word or act sublime, we must make it real.

The spirit will return and fill us.

He only is rightly immortal, to whom all things are immortal.

Fear God, and where you go, men shall think they walk in hallowed cathedrals.

∽

Of immortality, the soul when well employed is incurious.

There will be a new church founded on moral science.

I wish that life should not be cheap, but sacred.

∽

Mankind divides itself into two classes,—benefactors and malefactors.

Into every beautiful object there enters somewhat immeasurable and divine.

∽

A good symbol is the best argument, and is a missionary to persuade thousands.

The invisible and imponderable is the sole fact.

A man's action is only a picture-book of his creed. He does after what he believes.

The Bible itself is like an old Cremona, it has been played upon by the devotion of thousands of years, until every word and particle is public and tunable.

∽

The narrow sectarian cannot read astronomy with impunity.

The inviolate soul is in perpetual telegraphic communication with the Source of events.

∽

The Divine Nature carries on its administration by good men.

Christianity brought a new wisdom. But learning depends on the learner.

All I have seen teaches me to trust the Creator for all I have not seen.

∽

All serious souls are better believers in the immortality than we can give grounds for.

A great integrity makes us immortal.

Nothing Divine dies. All good is eternally reproductive.

Every natural fact is a symbol of some spiritual fact.

All things with which we deal preach to us. What is a farm but a mute gospel?

◇

Of that ineffable essence which we call Spirit, he that thinks most will say least.

The Spirit only can teach.

The world proceeds from the same Spirit as the body of man.

◇

The knowledge of man is an evening knowledge, but that of God is a morning knowledge.

No man ever prayed heartily without learning something.

◇

Every spirit builds itself a house; and beyond its house a world; and beyond its world a heaven.

The principle of veneration never dies out.

Preaching is the expression of the moral sentiment in application to the duties of life.

It is the office of a true teacher to show us
that God is, not was; that He speaketh,
not spake.

Dare to love God without mediator or veil.

∽

There are persons not actors, not speakers,
but influences.

A man adorns himself with prayer and love,
as an aim adorns an action.

Let us worship the mighty and transcendent
Soul.

∽

Truth is always holy, holiness always wise.

We cannot describe the natural history of
the soul, but we know that it is divine.

Everything divine shares the self-existence
of Deity.

∽

Nor knowest thou what argument
Thy life to thy neighbour's creed has lent.

∽

Yet not for all his faith can see
Would I that cowlèd churchman be.

The word by seers or sibyls told,
In groves of oak or fanes of gold,
Still floats upon the morning wind,
Still whispers to the willing mind.

∽

Ever fresh the broad creation,
A Divine improvisation,
From the heart of God proceeds,
A single will, a million deeds.

∽

I am an organ in the mouth of God,
My prophecy the music of His lips.

∽

He is the axis of the star,
He is the sparkle of the spar,
He is the heart of every creature,
He is the meaning of each feature;
And His Mind is the sky,
Than all it holds more deep, more
      high.

∽

                    These gray crags
Not on crags are hung,
But beads are of a rosary,
On prayer and music strung.

Lowly faithful, banish fear,
  Right onward drive unharmed;
The port well worth the cruise is near,
  And every wave is charmed.

⌒

The silent organ loudest chants
The master's requiem.

⌒

Covetous death bereaved us all,
To aggrandize one funeral.

⌒

House and tenant go to ground,
Lost in God, in Godhead found.

⌒

I am not poor, but I am proud
  Of one inalienable right,
Above the envy of the crowd,—
  Thought's holy light.

⌒

Go, speed the stars of Thought
  On to their shining goals;—
The sower scatters broad his seed,
  The wheat thou strew'st be souls.

Draw if thou canst the mystic line
Severing rightly His from thine,
Which is human, which divine.

&

There is nothing else but God.
    Where'er I look
All things hasten back to Him,
Light is but His shadow dim.

SCIENCE

PHYSICS : ASTRONOMY : GEOLOGY
CHEMISTRY : GEOMETRY : MATHEMATICS
BIOLOGY : ZOOLOGY

SCIENCE

EVERY new mind is a new classification.

Polarity, or action and reaction, we meet in every part of Nature.

Whilst the world is dual, so is every one of its parts.

⌇

If you tax too high, the revenue will yield nothing.

Everything in Nature contains all the powers of Nature.

The world globes itself in a drop of dew.

The eye is the first circle, the horizon is the second.

⌇

There are no fixtures in Nature. The universe is fluid and volatile.

Everything looks permanent until its secret is known.

At last we discover our curve is a parabola whose arcs will never meet.

We are symbols and inhabit symbols.

Language is fossil poetry.

The path of things is silent.

All things swim and glitter.

There is an optical illusion about every person we meet.

Character is of a stellar and undiminishable greatness.

Everything in Nature is bipolar, or has a positive and negative pole.

❧

Like can only be known by like.

Rotation is the law of Nature.

Nature never spares the opium or nepenthe.

Scatter the seeds of science and of song, that the germs of love and benefit may be multiplied.

❧

A drop of water has the properties of the sea, but cannot exhibit a storm.

Every fact is related on one side to sensation, on the other to morals. Nothing so thin but has these two faces.

Keep cool; it will be all one a hundred years hence.

Each must stand on his own glass tripod if he would keep his electricity.

Heat puts you in right relation with magazines of facts.

ᴓ

Society exists by chemical affinity, and not otherwise.

All conversation is a magnetic experiment.

Hitch your wagon to a star.

Our temperaments differ in capacity of heat, or we boil at different degrees.

ᴓ

Wherever the polarities meet,—wherever the fresh moral sentiment, the instinct of freedom and duty, come in direct opposition to fossil conservatism and the thirst of gain,—the spark will pass.

ᴓ

Science has shown the great circles in which Nature works.

Air is matter subdued by heat.

All things are flowing, even those that seem immovable.

The adamant is always passing into smoke.

Nations burn with internal fire of thought and affection, which wastes while it works.

*

There is no porter like gravitation.

Men love to wonder, and that is the seed of our science.

The science of power is forced to remember the power of science.

*

It is the depth at which we live, and not at all the surface extension that imports.

We need tonics, but must have those that cost little or no reaction.

Of all the cordials known to us, the best, safest, and most exhilarating is society.

*

I prize the mechanics of conversation! 'Tis pulley and lever and screw.

I prize the good invention whereby everybody is provided with somebody who is glad to see him.

The best conversation is between two persons who can talk only to each other.

As caloric to matter, so is love to mind.

To the geologist the sea is the only firmament.

〜

Civilization is a reagent, and eats away the old traits.

A nobility of soldiers cannot keep down a commonalty of shrewd scientific persons.

〜

The best political economy is the care and culture of men.

Great estates are not sinecures if they are to be kept great.

A creative economy is the fuel of magnificence.

〜

We can only obey our own polarity.

People are born with the moral or with the material bias.

In science we have to consider two things,— power and circumstance.

G

A tube made of a film of glass can resist the shock of the ocean, if filled with the same water.

The smallest candle fills a mile with its rays, and the papillæ of a man run out to every star.

⌁

Everything is pusher and pushed; and matter and mind are in perpetual tilt and balance.

In astronomy is vast space, but no foreign system; in geology vast time, but the same laws as to-day.

⌁

Physical force has no value where there is nothing else.

The world is mathematical, and has no casualty in all its vast and flowing curve.

⌁

Incapacity of melioration is the only mortal distemper.

The eye obeys exactly the action of the mind.

If a man is off his centre, the eyes show it.

A self-poise belongs to every particle, and
a rectitude to every mind.

The globe is a battery, because every atom
is a magnet.

To a sound constitution the defect of another
is at once manifest.

∽

A high aim is curative, as well as arnica.

Good is a good doctor, but Bad is sometimes
a better.

The poisons are our principal medicines,
which kill the disease and save the
life.

∽

Bad times have a scientific value. We
learn geology the morning after the
earthquake.

Sanity consists in not being subdued by
your means.

∽

The human heart concerns us more than the
poring into microscopes.

A man is a fagot of thunderbolts. All the
elements pour through his system.

From a great heart magnetism flows inces-
santly to draw great events

It is health of constitution that makes the sparkle and the power of the eye.

The scientific whim is lurking in all corners.

❧

The edge of every surface is tinged with prismatic rays.

There is no chance and no anarchy in the universe.

All is system and gradation.

Thin or solid, everything is in flight.

❧

Science does not know its debt to imagination.

Geology itself is only chemistry with the element of time added.

The world is always equal to itself.

Science corrects the old creeds.

❧

Every mind has a new compass, a new North, a new direction of its own.

In inquiries respecting the laws of the world, and the frame of things, the highest reason is always the truest.

Every surmise and vaticination of the mind
    is entitled to a certain respect.

The near explains the far. The drop is a small
    ocean. A man is related to all Nature.

❧

Good is positive. Evil is merely privative.

You cannot jump from the ground without
    using the resistance of the ground.

It is God's world and mine; yours as much
    as you want, mine as much as I want.

❧

Government has been a fossil; it should be
    a plant.

Money is of no value; it cannot spend
    itself.—All depends on the skill of the
    spender.

None should be a governor who has not a
    talent for governing.

❧

What god is this imperial Heat,
Earth's prime secret, sculpture's seat?

❧

For the world was built in order,
    And the atoms march in tune;
Rhyme the pipe, and Time the warder,
    The Sun obeys them, and the Moon.

Spirit that lurks each form within,
Beckons to spirit of its kin;
Self-kindled every atom glows,
And hints the future which it owes.

❧

Who saw what ferns and palms were
    pressed
Under the tumbling mountain's breast,
In the safe herbal of the coal?

❧

The storm wind wove, the torrent span,
Where they were bid the rivers ran;
New slaves fulfilled the poet's dream,
Galvanic wire, strong-shouldered steam.

ART AND ARTIST

THE CREATOR AND HIS WORK
POWERS OF THE TRUE ARTIST
QUALITIES OF ART AND BEAUTY
INTERRELATIONSHIP OF ALL THE ARTS
INFLUENCE OF ART
WISDOM AND TASTE

ART AND ARTIST

ART actualizes thought.

Art is the path of the Creator to His work.

Without the great arts which speak to a sense of beauty, a man seems to me a poor naked, shivering creature.

❧

Beauty is the quality which makes to endure.

Beauty without grace is the hook without the bait.

Beautiful details we must have, or no artist.

The true artist has the planet for his pedestal.

❧

Him we call an artist, who shall play on an assembly of men as a master on the keys of a piano.

Art is a jealous mistress.

No performance is worth loss of geniality.

Our arts are happy hits.

There is a courage in the treatment of every art by a master,—the courage of genius.

The laws of each art are convertible into the laws of every other.

Every genuine work of art has as much reason for being as the earth and the sun.

We are all wise. The difference between persons is not in wisdom, but in art.

Art must not be a superficial talent.

Those who are esteemed umpires of taste are often selfish and sensual.

'Tis the privilege of Art,
Thus to play its cheerful part,
Man in Earth to acclimate,
And bend the exile to his fate.

Her beauty was of God. The Maker's hand
Yet rested on its work.

GENIUS & IMAGINATION

USES AND POWERS OF GENIUS
PENALTIES AND PRIVILEGES
INSPIRATION AND ENTHUSIASM
SKILL, TALENT, AND PERCEPTION
IMAGINATION AND FANCY
ORIGINALS AND QUOTATIONS

GENIUS & IMAGINATION

GENIUS is the power to labour better and more availably.— Deserve thy genius and exalt it.

Genius sheds wisdom like perfume.

Though the success of the market is in the reward, true success is the doing.

❧

See that you hold yourself fast by the intellect.

The power of mind is not mortification, but life.

What is genius but finer love, a love impersonal?

Genius is its own end.

❧

When thought is best, there is most of it.

The day is always his who works in it with serenity and great aims.

Each admirable genius is but a successful diver in that sea whose floor of pearls is all your own.

All the ways of culture and greatness lead to solitary imprisonment.

No great men are original.

The greatest genius is the most indebted man.

You cannot see the mountain near.

∾

The profound apprehension of the Present is Genius.

Genius looks forward; the eyes of man are set in his forehead.

∾

Man Thinking must not be subdued by his instruments.

All vigour is contagious, and when we see creation we also begin to create.

Nothing great and lasting can be done except by inspiration.

∾

Talent may frolic and juggle, genius realizes and adds.

True genius will liberate and add new senses.

All minds quote. Old and new make the warp and woof of every moment.

The originals are not original.

The act of imagination is ever attended by pure delight.

Fancy is a wilful, imagination a spontaneous act.

❧

Fancy amuses, imagination expands and exalts us.

Fancy aggregates, imagination animates.

Evermore in the world is this marvellous balance of beauty and disgust, magnificence and rats.

❧

In our life and culture everything is worked up and comes in use.

Genius works in sport, and goodness smiles to the last.

Power dwells with cheerfulness; hope puts us in a working mood.

❧

We must do what we must, and call it by the best names.

We have a debt to every great heart, to every fine genius.

We want the great genius only for joy.

All the geniuses are usually so ill assorted
and sickly, that one is ever wishing
them somewhere else.

~

Concert fires people to a certain fury of performance they can rarely reach alone.

Thought is the seed of action.

The quality of imagination is to flow, not
to freeze.

~

Skill to do comes of doing.

Judge of the splendour of a nation, by the
insignificance of great individuals in it.

Our perception far outruns our talent.

There can be no greatness without abandon-
ment.

~

We are the children of genius, the children
of virtue.

Work in every hour paid or unpaid, see
only that thou work.

The divine gift is ever the instant life, which
receives and uses and creates.

A certain enormity of culture makes a man
    invisible to his contemporaries.

He who aims high must dread an easy home
    and popular manners.

Every brave heart must treat society as a
    child, and never allow it to dictate.

☙

Manners are the happy way of doing things.

The basis of good manners is self-reliance.

Manners impress as they indicate real power.

We live amid surfaces, and the true art of
    life is to skate well on them.

☙

We aim above the mark to hit the mark.

We live in a system of approximations.

Every moment instructs us, and every object
    for wisdom is infused into every form.

General ideas are essences.

☙

Come see the North-wind's masonry,
The frolic architecture of the snow.

☙

Eldest mason, Frost, has piled
Swift cathedrals in the wild.

H

He thought it happier to be dead,
To die for Beauty, than live for bread

❧

He must be musical,
Tremulous, impressional,
Alive to gentle influence
Of landscape and of sky,
And tender to the spirit-touch
Of man's or maiden's eye.

❧

Unsure the ebb and flow of thought;
The moon comes back, the spirit not.

MUSIC AND POETRY

THE VOICE IN SPEECH AND SONG
A MUSICAL PARNASSUS
POET AND PHILOSOPHER
THE WORLD A POEM
POETRY SYMBOLICAL AND SPIRITUAL
MUSIC AND WINE : SONG AND FEAST
ECHOES AND OMENS

MUSIC AND POETRY

EVERY sound ends in music.
A good voice has a charm in speech as in song.

We are lovers of rhyme and return, period and musical reflection.

Music is the poor man's Parnassus.

Poetry is not Devil's wine, but God's wine.

∽

The poets are liberating gods. They are free and they make free.

Oh Poet! Thou art true land-lord! sea-lord! air-lord!

The true philosopher and the true poet are one; and a beauty which is truth, and a truth which is beauty, is the aim of both.

∽

The poet proposes Beauty as his main end, the philosopher Truth.

The critic, the philosopher, is a failed poet.

Poetry must be affirmative. It is the piety of the intellect.

Poetry is the consolation of mortal men.

We have come into a world which is a living
    poem.

❧

Poetry is the perpetual endeavour to express
    the spirit of the thing.

A symbol always stimulates the intellect,
    therefore is poetry ever the best read-
    ing.

A beautiful woman is a practical poet.

❧

Poetry and prudence should be coincident.

Poetry if perfected is the only verity.

The poet is never the poorer for his song.

❧

    The music that can deepest reach,
    And cure all ill, is cordial speech.

❧

      Wine which music is,—
      Music and wine are one.

❧

    Chief of song where poets feast
    Is the wind-harp which thou seest
    In the casement at my side.

❧

    Echo waits with art and care,
    And will the faults of song repair.

Men consort in camp and town,
But the poet dwells alone.

✑

Delicate omens traced in air,
To the lone bard true witness bear.

✑

Thou canst not wave thy staff in air,
Or dip thy paddle in the lake,
But it carves the bow of beauty there,
And the ripples in rhymes the oar forsake.

✑

The quaking earth did quake in rhyme,
Seas ebbed and flowed in epic chime.

✑

'Twas the vintage day of field and wood,
When magic-wine for bards is brewed.

PAINTING & LITERATURE

PAINTING & LITERATURE

GREAT is paint; nay, God is the painter.

Nature paints the best part of the picture.

The artist has always the masters in his eye, although he affect to flout them.

∽

Every artist was first an amateur.

As the eye is the best composer, so light is the first of painters.

There is no object so foul that intense light will not make beautiful.

The masters painted for joy, and knew not that virtue had gone out of them.

∽

All great actions have been simple, and all great pictures are.

Art is not yet come to its maturity.

The best pictures can easily tell us their last secret.

Thought is the pent air-ball which can rive the planet.

123

The cat and the deer cannot move or sit inelegantly.

Beauty rests on necessities.

The line of beauty is the result of perfect economy.

It is proof of high culture to say the greatest matters in the simplest way.

Love the day. Do not leave the sky out of your landscape.

If thought is form, sentiment is colour.

Beauty is the mark God sets upon virtue.

Shakespeare was the master of revels to mankind.

Shakespeare is made up of important passages, like Damascus steel made up of old nails.

Every book is a quotation.

Great geniuses have the shortest biographies.

'Tis the good reader that makes the good book.

Men are born to write. All that can be thought can be written, first or last.

The wonder of the book is its superior intelligence.

∽

Talent alone cannot make a writer. There must be a man behind the book!

The life of man is the true romance.

No sentence will hold the whole truth.

Cut these words and they would bleed; they are vascular and alive.

∽

Knowledge is the knowing that we cannot know.

There *are* books,—and it is practicable to read them, because they are so few!

We prize books, and they prize them most who are themselves wise.

∽

Books are for the scholar's idle times.

One must be an inventor to read well.

The virtue of books is to be readable, and of orators to be interesting.

Each man of thought is surrounded by wiser men than he, if they cannot write as well.

He that writes to himself, writes to an eternal public.

❦

High behaviour is as rare in fiction as in fact.

Society is the stage on which manners are shewn, novels are their literature.

Society is a troop of thinkers, and the best heads among them take the best places.

❦

The scholar must embrace solitude as a bride.

Think alone and all places are friendly and sacred.

Inspiration makes solitude anywhere.

❦

We must be at the top of our condition to understand anything rightly.

The invariable mark of wisdom is to see the miraculous in the common.

Each age, it is found, must write its own books.

Books are the best of things, well used; abused, among the worst.

Good criticism is very rare, and always precious.

❦

Originality is being one's self, and reporting accurately what we see and are.

Literature idealizes action.

The simplest utterances are worthiest to be written.

❦

In every work of genius we recognize our own rejected thoughts.

Next to the originator of a good sentence is the first quoter of it.

The profit of a book is according to the sensibility of the reader.

❦

A writer appears to more advantage in the pages of another book than in his own.

Many men can write better under a mask than for themselves.

The first lesson of history is the good of evil.

A happy symbol is a sort of evidence that your thought is just.

There is no finer ear than Tennyson's, nor
    more command of the keys of language.

                       ∽

Certain ideas are in the air. We are all
    impressionable, for we are made of
    them.

Every writer is a skater, and must go partly
    where he would, and partly where the
    skates carry him.

                       ∽

Write that I may know you.   Style betrays
    you as your eyes do.

'Tis an economy of time to read old and
    famed books.

The famed books contain the best thoughts
    and facts.

What is really best in any book is translatable.

                       ∽

     Line in Nature is not found,
     Unit and universe are round.

                       ∽

    The tongue is prone to lose the way ;
     Not so the pen, for in a letter
    We have not better things to say,
     But surely say them better.

AGRICULTURE

AGRICULTURE

ALL our progress is an unfolding, like the vegetable bud.

Flowers and fruits are always fit presents.

The tempered light of the woods is stimulating and heroic.

All historic nobility rests on possession and use of land.

The farmer's office is precise and important. He represents the necessities.

The city is always recruited from the country.

Every plant is a manufacturer of soil.

Who are the farmer's servants? Geology and chemistry!

There are more belongings to every creature than his air and his food.

Each man, like each plant, has his parasites.

The longer the drought lasts, the more is the atmosphere surcharged with water.

No land is bad, but land is worse. If a man own land the land owns him.

To every plant there are two powers; one shoots down as rootlet, one upwards as tree.

One would say of the force in the works of Nature, all depends on the battery.

∽

The uses of the woods are many, and some of them for the scholar high and peremptory.

A cultivated labourer is worth many untaught labourers.

In the woods we return to reason and faith.

∽

The greatest delight which the fields and woods minister, is the suggestion of an occult relation between man and the vegetable.

A garden has this advantage, that it makes it indifferent where you live.

Punishment is a fruit that unsuspected ripens within the flower of the pleasure that concealed it.

∽

I am a willow of the wilderness,
Loving the wind that bent me.   All my hurts
My garden spade can heal

In thousand far-transplanting grafts
The parent fruit survives;
So in the new-born millions
The perfect Adam lives.

∽

Here once the embattled farmers stood,
And fired the shot heard round the world.

∽

And dulcimer mosquitoes in the woods
Hum their sly secrets in unwilling ears,
Which, like all gossip, leave a smart behind.

GEOGRAPHY & TRAVEL

SHIPPING AND SEA LIFE
MIND, HEART, AND SAILOR
ENGLAND AND THE SAXON RACE
WORLD-SECRETS AND PLEASURE
THE MEDICINE OF TRAVEL
INVENTORS AND DISCOVERERS
MAGICAL IRON

GEOGRAPHY & TRAVEL

THE voyage of the best ship is a zigzag line of a hundred tacks.

That country is fairest which is inhabited by the noblest minds.

Every ship is a romantic object, except that we sail in.

Every roof is agreeable to the eye until it is lifted.

The longest wave is quickly lost in the sea.

The most advanced nations are always those who navigate the most.

Wherever snow falls there is usually civil freedom.

Civilization depends on morality.

The sea life is an acquired taste, like that for tomatoes and olives.

The wonder is always new that any sane man can be a sailor.

A great mind is a good sailor, as a great heart is.

A voyage is one of the severest tests to try a man.

England is a garden.   Nothing is left as it
was made.

To see England well needs a hundred years.

The best nations are those most widely
related.

∽

Learn to swim, trim your bark, and the
wave which drowned it will be cloven
by it.

Cold and sea will train an imperial Saxon
race, which Nature cannot bear to lose.

The secret of the world is the tie between
person and event.   Person makes event,
and event person.

The pleasure of life is according to the man
that lives it.

Life is an ecstasy.

∽

Coal is a portable climate.   It carries the
heat of the tropics to Labrador and the
polar circle.

As a medical remedy travel seems one of
the best.

That we are here, is proof we ought to be
here.

Though we travel the world over to find the beautiful, we must carry it with us or we find it not.

Whenever we are wise, the whole world is wise and emblematic.

The world exists for thought.

❧

Turnpike is one thing, and blue sky another.

We are all inventors, each sailing out on a voyage of discovery, guided each by a private chart.

The world belongs to the energetic man. His will gives him new eyes.

❧

It is in vain to make a paradise but for good men.

We are not built like a ship to be tossed, but like a house to stand.

Railroad iron is a magician's rod, in its power to evoke the sleeping energies of land and water.

❧

What is it to sail o'er the calm blue sea,
To ride as a cloud o'er the purple floor
   With golden mists for company?

Sea full of food, the nourisher of kinds,
Purger of earth, and medicine of men.

Chambers of the great are jails,
And head-winds right for royal sails.

Sleep on, ye drowsy tribes whose old repose
The roaring oceans of the East enclose,—
Old Asia,—nurse of man and bower of gods.